THE WRONG SHEEP

ANGELA PARKER

ISBN: 978-1-7635330-6-6

Story and design by Angela Parker.

'Hi.

I'm a sheep.'

'The most awesome one, I think.'

'I'm also different.
Which makes me the wrong one.'

'But it also makes me special.'

'I stand out in a crowd.'

'And not because I love water slides.'

'The other sheep don't like my friends.'

'Or my style.'

'No one can find me in the dark.'

'Everyone keeps asking me if I have any wool.'

'Touch my wool. It's super soft.'

'Go on, touch it.'

'You touched my butt.'

‘It can be lonely being different...’

'No one picks me for a dance.'

'People don't like counting me to fall asleep.'

'My coat gets waterlogged.'

‘No one even likes my wool because it’s hard to dye.’

'Not even cats.'

'Stupid cats.'

'Don't be silly. This ones a unicorn-cat.'

'Pay attention.'

'During thunderstorms I look like this.'

'The other sheep generally avoid me.'

'It's impossible to have a conversation from this distance.'

'Unless I use my phone, obviously.'

'You wanna know how I charge it?

Where all good livestock charge their phones:

In a bush.'

'Don't ask stupid questions.'

'I just don't like to go with the crowd.'

'Plus, grass is GROSS.'

'Super Gross.'

'But the best thing about me?
The thing I'm just so,

So,

'So,

'Awesome at?'

'Sky diving.'

www.ingramcontent.com/pod-product-compliance
Lightning Source LLC
Chambersburg PA
CBHW042128030726
47599CB00002B/389

9781763533066